DIKEMBE MUTOMBO
DOLPH SCHAYES
CHARLES BARKLEY
WILT CHAMBERLAIN
FRED CARTER
GEORGE McGINNIS
JULIUS ERVING
MAURICE CHEEKS
BILLY CUNNINGHAM
HAL GREER
ALLEN IVERSON

MOSES MALONE

CREATIVE C EDUCATION

MICHAEL E. GOODMAN

Published by Creative Education, 123 South Broad Street, Mankato, MN 56001

Creative Education is an imprint of The Creative Company.

Designed by Rita Marshall

Photos by Allsport, AP/Wide World, Rich Kane, NBA Photos, SportsChrome

Library of Congress Cataloging-in-Publication Data

Goodman, Michael E. The history of the Philadelphia 76ers / by Michael E. Goodman.

p. cm. — (Pro basketball today)   ISBN 1-58341-109-7

1. Philadelphia 76ers (Basketball team)—History—

Juvenile literature. [1. Philadelphia 76ers (Basketball team)—History.

2. Basketball—History.] I. Title. II. Series.

GV885.52.P45 G65 2001   796.323'64'0974811—dc21   00-047337

First Edition 9 8 7 6 5 4 3 2 1

EVEN
THOUGH ITS
NAME IS GREEK (MEANING

"CITY OF BROTHERLY LOVE") AND ITS FOUNDERS WERE

British, Philadelphia, Pennsylvania, is American through and through.

Philadelphia is where the Declaration of Independence was signed in

1776, where Benjamin Franklin established America's first public library

and newspaper, and where Betsy Ross sewed the first American flag.

Philadelphia is also the home of some of America's oldest profes-

sional sports franchises—the Phillies in baseball, the Eagles in football,

the Flyers in hockey, and the 76ers in basketball. The 76ers, whose name

is symbolic of Philadelphia's place in American history, have put togeth-

AL BIANCHI

er a fascinating history of their own since joining the National

Basketball Association (NBA) in 1963.

Before his team became the 76ers, Dolph Schayes led Syracuse in scoring for 13 straight seasons.

{WARRIORS OUT, NATS IN} The history of pro basketball in Philadelphia actually began not with the 76ers, but with another team known as the Warriors. The Warriors were an original member of the Basketball Association of America (BAA), formed in 1946, and won the league's first championship. When the BAA merged with another league in 1949 to form the NBA, the Philadelphia Warriors became a charter member of the NBA as well.

The Warriors played in Philadelphia for 14 years, then decided to move to San Francisco in 1962. A year later, the Syracuse Nationals, a former rival of the Warriors in the NBA's Eastern Division, relocated to Philadelphia and became the 76ers.

CHARLES BARKLEY

Hal Greer's uncanny scoring ability made him one of the NBA's top guards.

HAL GREER

The new team was led by two future Hall-of-Famers who had come over from Syracuse: high-scoring guard Hal Greer and hardworking forward Dolph Schayes. The 6-foot-9 Schayes, a perennial NBA All-Star, was famous for his energy and determination. "I didn't have much speed, but I felt that by constantly moving, I could free myself, so I moved in and out all during the game," explained Schayes. "I kept pushing myself. I saw myself never getting tired."

John Kerr was the 76ers' first dominant rebounder, snagging 12 boards a game in **1963–64**.

Schayes served as a player-coach during the 1963–64 season and then devoted himself just to coaching the 76ers the next two years. His teams made the playoffs all three seasons, thanks in large part to Greer. Greer was a deadly accurate jump shooter who even jumped before releasing the ball when he shot free throws. He was the club leader in every offensive category except rebounding, which was the domain of

JOHN KERR

Center Theo Ratliff followed in Wilt Chamberlain's footsteps as a top shot blocker.

THEO RATLIFF

veteran center John Kerr and young forward Chet Walker.

{CHAMBERLAIN AND A CHAMPIONSHIP} The 76ers were

Guard Larry Costello helped the 76ers capture their first Eastern Division title in 1965–66.

successful, but they weren't a championship-caliber team yet. That all changed when the club made a blockbuster trade for an old Philadelphia hero, Wilt Chamberlain. Local fans were very familiar with Chamberlain, who had been a Philadelphia high school star and played several seasons with the Warriors before they moved west. The 7-foot-1 giant was one of the greatest scorers and rebounders in NBA history, and Philly fans were thrilled to see the "Big Dipper" return home in 1965.

With Chamberlain in the lineup and backed by Greer, Walker, and power forward Luke Jackson, the 76ers were transformed from an average team to a true championship contender. Still, the club needed another consistent scorer and rebounder.

BILLY CUNNINGHAM

That player, Billy Cunningham, arrived in Philadelphia via the

1966 NBA Draft. Cunningham was a 6-foot-7 forward from the

University of North Carolina. Nicknamed the "Kangaroo Kid" for his

great jumping ability and aggressiveness, Cunningham brought new fire

to the 76ers lineup that opened the 1966–67 season.

Under new coach Alex Hannum, the club won 45 of its first 49 games and finished with a 68–13 record. That was the best mark in

NBA history up to that time. But the 76ers didn't stop there. They

Posting their best home record ever, the mighty 76ers went 28–2 in Philadelphia in **1966–67**.

breezed by the Cincinnati Royals and Boston Celtics in

the first two rounds of the playoffs, then wrapped up the

NBA title by trouncing Chamberlain's old team—the San

Francisco Warriors—in six games. At last, Wilt had helped

bring an NBA title home to Philadelphia.

{THE BIG FALL} The 76ers continued on in 1967–68 as if their

championship year had never ended. They finished the season with a

62–20 record, eight games ahead of Boston, and seemed primed to

replace the aging Celtics as the NBA's most dominant team. Then a

strange thing happened. The Celtics, led by Bill Russell and John

Havlicek, roared back from a three-games-to-one deficit to beat the

76ers in the Eastern Conference Finals and then captured their 10th

WILT CHAMBERLAIN

NBA championship in 12 years. The 76ers were crushed and demoralized by their unexpected defeat.

The loss triggered a chain of events that sent the 76ers into a

terrible downward spiral. First, Coach Hannum resigned to join the

newly formed American Basketball Association (ABA). Next,

Chamberlain expressed discontent with the team and was traded to the

Lakers for cash and three players. Cunningham led the 76ers to one last

playoff appearance after the 1968–69 season, and then the club went

through a six-year free fall.

Philadelphia hit rock bottom in 1972–73. Before

that season began, Cunningham signed with an ABA

team, and the Sixers were left without a leader. At one

point that year, Philadelphia lost a league-record 20 games

in a row. The team finished with a humiliating 9–73 mark, still the

worst record in NBA history.

The 76ers stayed in the Eastern Division cellar for three straight

seasons. The club's lineup during those years consisted mostly of aging

veterans and journeymen and featured only one legitimate scoring

threat—a speedy guard named Fred Carter, whose reckless and aggressive

style of play earned him the nickname "Mad Dog." Immediate help was

Guard Doug Collins's offensive fire-power helped the 76ers rebound from a disastrous **1972–73**.

DOUG COLLINS

needed to rejuvenate the once-proud team.

{HELP ARRIVES FROM THE ABA} During their fall, the 76ers

Few NBA forwards in the '70s could match the strength of the 76ers' George McGinnis.

had suffered some key defections to the ABA. It was fitting, therefore, that three former ABA stars helped turn the club around. First on the scene was power forward George McGinnis, who jumped from the ABA's Indiana Pacers to the 76ers in 1975. A former ABA Most Valuable

Player, "Big George" quickly proved that he could be a star in the NBA as well. In his first season in Philadelphia, McGinnis led the 76ers in scoring, rebounding, and steals and was second in assists and blocked shots.

A year later, the Sixers made an even more impressive acquisition from the ABA when they purchased the contract of Julius "Dr. J" Erving from the financially troubled New Jersey Nets. With his amazing fakes and soaring dunks, Erving was the man who truly brought attention to

GEORGE McGINNIS

the ABA during his years with the Nets. Said ABA commissioner Dave

DeBusschere, a former NBA star himself, "There are athletes who are

known as 'the franchise,' but Julius isn't the franchise—he's the league!"

Erving's arrival was a real turning point for the 76ers. During

the 11 years he wore a Philadelphia uniform, the 76ers never suffered a

losing record. Erving and McGinnis led the 76ers to the Eastern

Conference crown in 1976–77. But their championship hopes were ended

by Bill Walton and the Portland Trail Blazers in the 1977 NBA Finals.

The following year, Billy Cunningham returned to

Philadelphia, this time as the club's new head coach. In a

key move, Cunningham traded McGinnis to the Denver

Nuggets for forward Bobby Jones. Jones was the ultimate

team player. He could have been a fine scorer, but he

chose instead to concentrate unselfishly on defense and rebounding. For

10 straight seasons (eight of them with the 76ers), Jones was named to

the NBA's All-Defensive team.

Cunningham added one more key player via the 1978 NBA

Draft—a 6-foot-3 point guard named Maurice "Mo" Cheeks from West Texas

State. Cunningham made Cheeks the floor general of Philadelphia's

high-powered offense. The Sixers squads of the late 1970s and early '80s

HENRY BIBBY

Maurice Cheeks led the 76ers in assists and steals for 10 straight seasons.

MAURICE CHEEKS

won with great consistency during the regular season, yet they always came up short in the NBA playoffs.

{MOSES MAKES THE DIFFERENCE} Following the 1982 playoffs, the 76ers traded with the Houston Rockets for center Moses Malone. Some critics wondered whether Malone, a two-time NBA MVP, would be able to share the spotlight with Erving. But Erving had no such doubts. "At this point, winning the title is the only thing that's on my mind," said Dr. J, "and there's no question that Moses can help us get there. . . . I'm proud to be playing at his side."

Side by side, Erving and Malone powered the Sixers to 65 victories during the 1982–83 season and then to the NBA championship over the Los Angeles Lakers. Malone was named MVP of both the regular season and the playoffs, and Erving proudly hoisted the NBA championship

Moses Malone was one of four Philadelphia players named to the **1983** All-Star Game.

MOSES MALONE

trophy over his head while Philadelphia fans celebrated.

It was a fleeting moment of glory, however. The 76ers maintained

winning records for a few more years, but they never challenged for

another title. Then Malone was traded away, and Erving and Jones

retired. Soon, only Cheeks was left from the 76ers' championship squad,

but he was not alone as the club leader. Joining him was one of the most unusual talents in NBA history: forward Charles Barkley.

The 6-foot-5 and 280-pound Barkley, drafted in 1984, looked more like a football lineman than a basketball star, but he quickly proved that looks can be deceiving. He was a fierce competitor who outfought and outjumped taller opponents. He also outtalked them, never lacking something interesting to say. During eight seasons in Philadelphia, "Sir Charles" averaged 23 points and nearly 12 rebounds per game.

In **1990–91**, Rick Mahorn's rebounding helped the team post its 15th winning mark in 16 seasons.

Unfortunately, Barkley's supporting cast in those years—backcourt players such as Hersey Hawkins and Johnny Dawkins and frontcourt partners Mike Gminski, Armon Gilliam, and Rick Mahorn—was solid but unspectacular. The 76ers were slowly overtaken by other teams in the Eastern Conference, and the club's record drifted below .500. The losing frustrated Barkley, who asked to be traded in 1992.

RICK MAHORN

{ALLEN IS THE ANSWER} With Barkley gone, the 76ers sank even lower. Top draft picks such as centers Shawn Bradley and Sharone Wright never panned out, and the club hit rock bottom during the 1995–96 campaign, finishing with a miserable 18–64 record. That was the bad news. The good news was that the 76ers' poor finish gave them the right to pick first in the 1996 NBA Draft, and they selected

Georgetown point guard Allen Iverson. Nicknamed "the Answer," Iverson brashly announced that he planned to be the answer to Philadelphia's quest for another NBA title.

Iverson backed up his talk with action. The lightning-quick guard proved that he could break down opposing defenses better than anyone else in the league. "I try to put pressure on the defense, try to create things for my teammates and myself," Iverson explained. "I am always,

Sniper Dana Barros established a team record with 197 three-point baskets in **1994–95**.

28

DANA BARROS

always looking to score, always looking to make something happen on

the court." Iverson's amazing offensive skills and 23-points-per-game

average helped him capture the NBA Rookie of the Year

award in 1996–97.

Then, before the 1997–98 season, the 76ers per-

suaded longtime NBA coach Larry Brown to come to

Philly to rebuild the club around Iverson. The coach and

young guard, both with strong egos, had some difficulties getting along

at first. But they realized that they both had the same goal and slowly

began working together to achieve it.

Brown helped engineer key trades and free agent signings that

brought to Philadelphia such players as centers Matt Geiger and Theo

Ratliff; forwards Tyrone Hill, Toni Kukoc, and George Lynch; and point

guard Eric Snow. He then began molding them into a cohesive unit. It

Forward Clarence Weatherspoon headed the 76ers' rebounding efforts in the late **'90s**.

CLARENCE WEATHERSPOON

Sensational
guard Allen
Iverson led
a rising
Philadelphia
squad into the
21st century.

ALLEN IVERSON

Dikembe Mutombo, the most feared shot blocker in the NBA, guarded the lane.

DIKEMBE MUTOMBO

all began to come together in 1998–99. Iverson won the NBA scoring title that season—becoming the first 76ers player to do so since Wilt Chamberlain—but he also began to play more within Coach Brown's team concept. As a result, the 76ers returned to the playoffs for the first of three straight seasons. In 2001, the team furthered its drive for an NBA crown by trading for All-Star center Dikembe Mutombo.

With the help of guard Eric Snow, Philadelphia bolted to an NBA-best 36–14 start in **2000–01**.

The Philadelphia 76ers have put together a long and proud history in the NBA and are more than ready to establish their rightful position as one of the league's elite teams. Another NBA championship may be on the horizon for the 76ers, and faithful Philadelphia fans think that's a revolutionary idea.

ERIC SNOW